Apples of Gold

Jo Pett

A sp   ction   hundreds of famou   serious,   nd inspirational   subje   as Love, Joy, I   ng,   tleness, Good   tty a spent over t   these wonderful s   the compiler of many   ks. In its original editio   OLD has sold millic   es a   particularly treasu   erful g

"A   fitly s   n is like apples of

in   silver."

—Proverbs 25:11

APPLES OF GOLD

Compiled by Jo Petty

Phoenix Press

WALKER AND COMPANY
New York

Large Print Edition published by
arrangement with C. R. Gibson Company

8/90   DAV.TIT 6.12

Printed in the United States of America

Library of Congress Cataloging in Publication Data
Main entry under title:

Apples of gold.

    Reprint. Originally published: 1962.
    1. Quotations, English. 2. Large type
books. I. Petty, Jo.
[PN6081.A66 1985]   082   85-6363
ISBN 0-8027-2502-3 (Walker : lg. print)

First Large Print Edition, 1985
Walker and Company
720 Fifth Avenue
New York, New York 10019

But the fruit of the Spirit is love,
joy, peace, long suffering, gentleness,
goodness, faith, meekness, temperance:
against such there is no law.

—Galatians 5:22–23

A word fitly spoken
is like apples of gold
in pictures of silver.

Proverbs 25:11

Contents

Love 1

Joy 18

Peace 46

Long suffering 57

Gentleness 75

Goodness 79

Faith 91

Meekness 111

Temperance 125

⚭

The material in this book has
been collected over a long period
of time. Many of the original
sources are unknown to the compiler.
The compiler wishes to acknowledge
the original authors, whoever they
may be, but has confidence that
they would urge, with her, "Do not
inquire as to who said this, but
pay attention to what is said."

⚭

Love

Scientists know only what love does. Love, properly applied, could virtually empty our asylums, our prisons, our hospitals. Love is the touchstone of psychiatric treatment. Love can be fostered, extended, used to subjugate hate and thus cure diseases. More and more clearly every day, out of biology, anthropology, sociology, history, economics, psychology, the plain common sense, the necessary mandate of survival—that we love our neighbors as ourselves—is being confirmed and reaffirmed. Christ gave us only one commandment—Love . . . Now to the laboratory with love!

———

Where love is, there God is.

———

Love

To love is virtually to know; to know is not virtually to love.

———

Real friends are those who, when you've made a fool of yourself, don't feel that you've done a permanent job.

———

We may give without loving, but we cannot love without giving.

———

Work is love made visible.

———

It also takes two to make up after a quarrel.

———

Faults are thick when love is thin.

———

To love life through labor is to be intimate with life's inmost secret.

———

Do not judge your friend until you stand in his place.

———

He who sows courtesy reaps friendship,
and he who plants kindness gathers love.

———

You shall judge a man by his foes as well
as by his friends.

———

Adolescence is the age at which children
stop asking questions because they know
all the answers.

———

Except in occasional emergencies there is
not much that one man can do for
another, other than to help him to help
himself.

———

The door to the human heart can be
opened only from the inside.

———

Friendship is to be purchased only by
friendship.

———

Let us be the first to give a friendly sign,
to nod first, smile first, speak first,

Love

and—if such a thing is necessary—
forgive first.

———

The light of friendship is like the light of
phosphorus, seen when all around is
dark.

———

I did a favor yesterday,
  A kindly little deed . . .
And then I called to all the world
  To stop and look and heed.
They stopped and looked and
    flattered me
  In words I could not trust,
And when the world had gone away
  My good deed turned to dust.

A very tiny courtesy
  I found to do today;
'Twas quickly done, with none to
    see.
  And then I ran away . . .
But Someone must have witnessed it,
  For—truly I declare—

As I sped back the stony path
  Roses were blooming there!

———

Restraint without love is barbarity.
Love without restraint commits
  suicide.

———

For we must share if we would keep
  That blessing from above;
Ceasing to give, we cease to have,
  Such is the law of love.

———

If a single man achieves the highest kind
of love, it will be sufficient to neutralize
the hate of millions.

———

Love cannot be wasted. It makes no
difference where it is bestowed, it always
brings in big returns.

———

God pardons like a mother, who kisses
the offense into everlasting forgetfulness.

———

To handle yourself, use your head;
To handle others, use your heart.

———

Love

Measure your life by loss instead of gain;
not by the wine drunk, but in the wine
poured forth, for love's strength stands
in love's sacrifice; and who suffers most
has most to give.

———

The only safe and sure way to destroy an
enemy is to make him your friend.

———

Are you lonely, O my brother?
Share your little with another!
Stretch a hand to one unfriended,
And your loneliness is ended.

———

The only greatness is unselfish love.

———

Return to him who does you wrong your
purest love, and he will cease from doing
wrong; for love will purify the heart of
him who is beloved as truly as it purifies
the heart of him who loves.

———

Creation of woman from the rib of man:
She was not made of his head to top him;

nor out of his feet to be trampled upon by him; but out of his side to be equal with him; under his arm, to be protected; and near his heart to be beloved.

———

A foreigner is a friend I haven't met yet.

———

The only way to have a friend is to be one.

———

It is only the forgiving who are qualified to receive forgiveness.

———

> The father is the head of the house—
> The mother is the heart of the house.

———

The love you liberate in your work is the love you keep.

———

How seldom we weigh our neighbor in the same balance with ourselves.

———

Love

A friend is a person with whom you dare to be yourself.

———

Add all the love of all the parents and the total sum cannot be multiplied enough times to express God's love for me, the least of his children.

———

A long life is barely enough for a man and a woman to understand each other; and to be understood is to love. The man who understands one woman is qualified to understand pretty well everything.

———

Not the quarry, but the chase,
Not the trophy, but the race.

———

Love is not soft like water, it is hard like rock, on which the waves of hatred beat in vain.

———

It is in loving, not in being loved, the heart is blessed; It is in giving, not in seeking gifts, we find our quest;

Whatever be your longing or your need,
that give; So shall your soul be fed, and
you indeed shall live.

———

To learn and never be filled, is wisdom;
To teach and never be weary is love.

———

Conscience is God's presence in man.

———

> Mrs.—Do you love me still?
> Mr.—Yes, better than any other
> way.

———

God regards the greatness of the love that
prompts the man, rather than the
greatness of his achievement.

———

It is as absurd to pretend that one cannot
love the same woman always as to
pretend that a good artist needs several
violins to play a piece of music.

———

I married her because we have so many
faults in common.

———

9

Love

We like someone because. We love someone although.

———

A friend is one who knows all about you and still likes you.

———

Go often to the house of your friend, for weeds choke up the unused path.

———

Your friend has a friend, and your friend's friend has a friend; be discreet.

———

He that cannot forgive others breaks the bridge over which he must pass, for every man has need to be forgiven.

———

Forgiveness is the fragrance the violet sheds on the heel that crushed it.

———

To understand is to pardon.

———

Friendship is the only cement that will ever hold the world together.

———

Always forgive your enemies; nothing annoys them so much.

———

Love is the passionate and abiding desire on the part of two or more people to produce together conditions under which each can be, and spontaneously express, his real self; to produce together an intellectual soil and an emotional climate in which each can flourish, far superior to what either could achieve alone.

———

The best way for a husband to clinch an argument is to take her in his arms.

———

The bonds of matrimony aren't worth much unless the interest is kept up.

———

A friend is a present you give yourself.

———

One reason why a dog is such a lovable creature is that his tail wags instead of his tongue.

———

Love

Come what may, hold fast to *love*! Though men should rend your heart, let them not embitter or harden it. We win by tenderness; we conquer by forgiveness.

———

One of the mysteries of life is how the boy who wasn't good enough to marry the daughter can be the father of the smartest grandchild in the world.

———

Friends are made by many acts—and lost by only one.

———

Pure religion is love in action.

———

The smallest good deed is better than the grandest intention.

———

I've found a little remedy
  To ease the life we live
And make each day a happier one—
  It is the word "forgive."

So often little things come up
   That leave a pain and sting,
That covered up at once would not
   Amount to anything.

'Tis when we hold them up to view,
   And brood and sulk and fret,
They greater grow before our eyes;
   'Twere better to forget.

———

Politeness is a small price to pay for the good will and affection of others.

———

The greater the man, the greater the courtesy.

———

The coin of God's realm is love.

———

A partnership with God is motherhood.

———

It is better to have loved and lost than never to have loved at all.

———

Love

American Creed: Patriotism which leaps over the fence of party prejudice. Religion which jumps over the wall of intolerance. Brotherhood which climbs over the mountain of national separations.

———

The best gifts are tied with heartstrings.

———

Man is probably the only animal which even attempts to have anything to do with his half-grown young.

———

Every calling is great when greatly pursued.

———

An injurious truth has no merit over an injurious lie.

———

A friend is one who comes to you when all others leave.

———

> He drew a circle that shut me out,
> But love and I had the wit to win;

We drew a larger circle that took him
   in.

___

Mothers, as well as fools, sometimes
walk where angels fear to tread.

___

When a man does a noble act, date him
from that. Forget his faults. Let his
noble act be the standpoint from which
you regard him.

___

A mistake at least proves somebody
stopped talking long enough to do
something.

___

A teacher affects eternity; he can never
tell where his influence stops.

___

'Twas her thinking of others made you
think of her.

___

Water which is distant is no good for a
fire which is near.

___

Love

Success in marriage is much more than finding the right person; it is a matter of being the right person.

———

Hate is a prolonged manner of suicide.

———

Some women work so hard to make good husbands that they never quite manage to make good wives.

———

Put yourself in his place.

———

What counts is not the number of hours you put in, but how much you put in the hours.

———

Love sees through a telescope—not a microscope.

———

Some people give and forgive; others get and forget.

———

He makes no friends who never made a foe.

———

Women's styles may change, but their designs remain the same.

———

If you had to do it over, would you fall in love with yourself again?

———

A woman worries about the future until she gets a husband, while a man never worries about the future until he gets a wife.

———

Ceremonies are different in every country, but true politeness is everywhere the same.

∽

Joy

There is nothing I can give you which
you have not, but there is much that
while I cannot give you, you can take:
No heaven can come to us unless our
hearts find rest in it today. Take Heaven.
No peace lies in the future which is not
hidden in this present instant. Take
Peace.
The gloom of the world is but a shadow;
behind it, yet within reach, is joy. Take
Joy.

——

It is easy to be pleasant
    When life flows by like a song,
But the man worth while is one who
        will smile,
    When everything goes dead wrong.

For the test of the heart is trouble,
    And it always comes with the years,
And the smile that is worth the
        praises of earth
    Is the smile that shines thru the
        tears.

———

Keep your enthusiasms, and forget your birthdays—formula for youth!

———

Do you see *difficulties* in every *opportunity* or *opportunities* in every *difficulty?*

———

If you would know the greatest sum in addition, count your blessings.

———

Money and time are the heaviest burdens of life, and the unhappiest of all mortals are those who have more of either than they know how to use.

———

I can alter my life by altering my attitude of mind.

———

Joy

As torrents in summer, half dried in
   their channels,
Suddenly rise, 'tho the sky is still
   cloudless,
For rain has been falling far off at their
   fountains;
So hearts that are fainting grow full to
   o'erflowing,
And they that behold it marvel, and
   know not
That God at their fountains, so far off
   has been raining.

———

Happiness is possible only when one is
busy. The body must toil, the mind must
be occupied, and the heart must be
satisfied. Those who do good as
opportunity offers are sowing seed all the
time, and they need not doubt the
harvest.

———

Joy, temperance and repose
Slam the door on the doctor's nose.

———

One of the great arts of living is the art of forgetting.

―――――

He who would have nothing to do with thorns must never attempt to gather flowers.

―――――

Don't let the seeds spoil your enjoyment of a watermelon. Just spit out the seeds.

―――――

Little and often fills the purse.

―――――

You grow up the day you have your first real laugh—at yourself.

―――――

There is no place more delightful than one's own fireside.

―――――

When shall we all learn that the *good news* needs the telling, and that all men need to know?

―――――

Keep on your toes and you won't run down at the heels.

―――――

Joy

Interesting people are people who are interested. Bores are people who are bored.

———

Yes, it's pretty hard, the optimistic old woman admitted. I have to get along with only two teeth—one upper, one lower—but, thank goodness, they meet.

———

Some cause happiness wherever they go; others whenever they go.

———

Happiness is a perfume you cannot pour on others without getting a few drops on yourself.

———

I'm so glad I'm back home I'm glad I went.

———

I do not feel any age yet. There is no age to the spirit.

———

To what avail the plow or sail, or land, or life, if freedom fail?

———

To be without some of the things you want is an indispensable part of happiness.

_____

There are no uninteresting things, there are only uninteresting people.

_____

> I want a soul so full of joy—
> Life's withering storms cannot
>   destroy.

_____

Diner: "Do you serve crabs here?"
Waiter: "We serve anyone; sit down."

_____

The worst bankrupt in the world is the man who has lost his enthusiasm. Let him lose everything but enthusiasm and he will come through again to success.

_____

I have noticed that folks are generally about as happy as they have made up their minds to be.

_____

Joy

> If you want to be happy,
>   Begin where you are,
> Don't wait for some rapture
>   That's future and far.
> Begin to be joyous, begin to be glad
>   And soon you'll forget
> That you ever were sad.

―――――

Two tragedies in life: One is not to get your heart's desire. The other is to get it.

―――――

For all its terrors and tragedies . . . the life of man is a thing of potential beauty and dignity . . . To live is good.

―――――

I know what happiness is, for I have done good work.

―――――

Growing old is no more than a bad habit which a busy person has no time to form.

―――――

The only consistently bright life is the persistently right life.

―――――

What one has, one ought to use; and whatever he does he should do with all his might.

_____

One day as I sat musing
Alone and melancholy and without a
    friend,
There came a voice from out of the
    gloom,
Saying, "Cheer up! Things might be
    worse."
So I cheered up,
And sure enough—things got worse.

_____

It takes both rain and sunshine to make a rainbow.

_____

God does not deduct from man's allotted time those hours spent in *fishing*.

_____

An unfailing mark of a blockhead is the chip on his shoulder.

_____

Joy

Keep ascending the mountain of cheerfulness by daily scattering seeds of kindness along the way as best you can, and, should mists hide the mountaintop, continue undaunted and you will reach the sun-tipped heights in your own life-experience.

———

People are lonely because they build walls instead of bridges.

———

Let us realize that what happens round us is largely outside our control, but that the way we choose to react to it is inside our control.

———

Any person who is always feeling sorry for himself, should be.

———

All people smile in the same language.

———

The only way on earth to multiply happiness is to divide it.

———

How many smiles from day to day
I've missed along my narrow way!
How many kindly words I've lost
What joy has my indifference cost!
This glorious friend that now I know
Would have been friendly years ago.

———

It is not he who has little, but he who
wants more, who is poor.

———

A man's mind is like his car. If it gets to
knocking too much, he'd better have it
overhauled or change it.

———

One of the best things a man can have up
his sleeve is a funny-bone.

———

Never miss an opportunity to make
others happy, even if you have to let
them alone to do it.

———

Old age isn't so bad . . . when you
consider the alternative.

———

Joy

The really happy man is the one who can enjoy the scenery when he has to take a detour.

_____

Success is a bright sun that obscures and makes ridiculously unimportant all the little shadowy flecks of failure.

_____

The cost of a thing is that amount of life which must be exchanged for it.

_____

Mirth is from God, and dullness is from the devil. You can never be too sprightly, you can never be too good—tempered.

_____

Plan your work—work your plan.

_____

Change yourself and your work will seem different.

_____

Be cheerful. Of all the things you wear, your expression is the most important.

_____

To be happy ourselves is a most effectual contribution to the happiness of others.

———

I am born happy every morning.

———

So long as enthusiasm lasts, so long is youth still with us.

———

Apart from enthusiasm, joy cannot live.

———

The world belongs to the enthusiast who keeps cool.

———

Be a lamp in the chamber if you cannot be a star in the sky.

———

What sunshine is to flowers, smiles are to humanity.

———

If we fill our hours with regrets over the failures of yesterday, and with worries over the problems of tomorrow, we have no today in which to be thankful.

———

Joy

Blessed is the man who digs a well from which another may draw faith.

———

Spilled on this earth are all the joys of heaven.

———

The secret of being miserable is to have the leisure to bother about whether you are happy or not.

———

Always speak the truth and you'll never be concerned with your memory.

———

There is no duty we so much underrate as the duty of being happy.

———

Mind unemployed is Mind unenjoyed.

———

Just think how happy you'd be if you lost everything you have right now—and then got it back again.

———

Earth is crammed with heaven
And every common bush is afire with God.

———

Laugh a little—sing a little
  As you go your way!
Work a little—play a little,
  Do this every day!

Give a little—take a little,
  Never mind a frown—
Make your smile a welcomed thing
  All around the town!

Laugh a little—love a little,
  Skies are always blue!
Every cloud has silver linings,
  But it's up to you!

―――

If you ever find happiness by hunting for
it, you will find it, as the old woman did
her lost spectacles, safe on her nose all
the time.

―――

Remember that the coin you clutch has
never brought happiness.
The world and you will profit more from
sincere thoughtfulness.

―――

Joy

Happiness consists in activity—it is a running stream, not a stagnant pool.

――――

> They told him it couldn't be done.
> > With a smile, he went right to it.
> He tackled the thing that couldn't be
> > done
> And couldn't do it.

――――

May you live all the days of your life.

――――

When a man has a "pet peeve" it's remarkable how often he pets it.

――――

The real democratic American idea is not that every man shall be on a level with every other, but that every man shall have liberty, without hindrance, to be what God made him.

――――

He who receives a benefit with gratitude repays the first installment on his debt.

――――

If I keep a green bough in my heart, the singing bird will come.

――――

You have no more right to consume happiness without producing it than to consume wealth without producing it.

———

Cold and reserved natures should remember that, though not infrequently flowers may be found beneath the snow, it is chilly work to dig for them and few care to take the trouble.

———

Every man's work is a portrait of himself.

———

Economy makes happy homes and sound nations; instill it deep.

———

Things are pretty well evened up in this world.
Other people's troubles are not so bad as yours, but their children are a lot worse.

———

The office of government is not to confer happiness, but to give men opportunity to work out happiness for themselves.

———

Joy

If you would make a man happy, do not add to his possessions but subtract from the sum of his desires.

Why help to make the world a dreary
    place—
  Why be a rainy day?
Why harp on old mistakes that we
    regret?
  Why be a rainy day?
Why wear the dismal mask of
    hopelessness?
  Why be a rainy day?

Sorrow with his pick mines the heart, but he is a cunning workman. He deepens the channels whereby happiness may enter, and he hollows out new chambers for joy to abide in, when he is gone.

Children are a great comfort in your old age—and they help you reach it faster, too.

One great use of words is to hide our thoughts.

_____

Praise, like gold and diamonds, owes its value to its scarcity.

_____

Heaven is blessed with perfect rest, but the blessing of earth is toil.

_____

True happiness depends upon close alliance with God.

_____

To see God in everything makes life the greatest adventure there is.

_____

A thankful heart is not only the greatest virtue, but the parent of all the other virtues.

_____

Humdrum is not where you live; it's what you are.

_____

A sad saint is a sorry saint.

_____

Joy

Happiness is the best teacher of good manners; only the unhappy are churlish.

———

There is always something wrong with a man, as there is with a motor, when he knocks continually.

———

A Smile is Cheer to you and me
The cost is nothing—it's given free
It comforts the weary—gladdens the sad
Consoles those in trouble—good or bad
To rich and poor—beggar or thief
It's free to all of any belief
A natural gesture of young and old
Cheers on the faint—disarms the bold
Unlike most blessings for which we pray
It's one thing we keep when we give it away.

———

We must be willing to pay a price for

freedom, for no price that is ever asked for it is half the cost of doing without it.

———

O, I am grown so free from care since my heart broke!

———

Life and Death are parts of the same great adventure. Do not fear to die and do not shrink from the joy of life.

———

Sit ye, rock and think.

———

You may call that your own which no man can take from you.

———

Optimist or Pessimist? Do you call traffic signals go-lights?

———

Living is like licking honey off a thorn.

———

If we learn how to give ourselves, to forgive others, and to live with thanksgiving, we need not seek happiness—it will seek us.

———

Joy

Gratitude is the memory of the heart.

———

Sympathy is never wasted except when you give it to yourself.

———

No man has more time than I.

———

Better to light one candle than to curse the darkness.

———

The man who deals in sunshine is the man who wins the crowds.
He does a lot more business than the man who peddles clouds.

———

Visits always give pleasure—if not the coming, then the going.

———

Liberty is always dangerous, but it is the safest thing we have.

———

Winter on her head—Eternal spring in her heart.

———

All sunshine makes a desert.

_____

Joy is not in things, it is in us.

_____

Happiness is a thing to be practiced like a violin.

_____

That load becomes light which is cheerfully borne.

_____

Manners are the happy way of doing things.

_____

To be wronged is nothing unless you continue to remember it.

_____

Our joys are our wings;
Our sorrows are our spurs.

_____

The days that make us happy make us wise.

_____

There is nothing more beautiful than a rainbow, but it takes both rain and sunshine to make a rainbow. If life is to

Joy

be rounded and many-colored like the rainbow, both joy and sorrow must come to it. Those who have never known anything but prosperity and pleasure become hard and shallow, but those whose prosperity has been mixed with adversity become kind and gracious.

—————

Almost all men improve on acquaintance.

—————

Happiness consists not in possessing much, but in being content with what we now possess. He who wants little always has enough.

—————

The smile on your face is the light in the window that tells people that you are at home.

—————

The secret of happy living is not to do what you like but to like what you do.

—————

If you don't make a living, live on what you make.

—————

If we pause to think, we will have cause to thank.

———

Some men have their first dollar.
The man who is really rich is one who still has his first friend.

———

Once upon a time I planned to be
  An artist of celebrity.
A song I thought to write one day,
  And all the world would homage
    pay.
I longed to write a noted book,
  But what I did was—learn to cook.
For life with simple tasks is filled,
  And I have done, not what I willed,
Yet when I see boys' hungry eyes
  I'm glad I make good apple pies!

———

The way to be happy is to make others happy.
Helping others is the secret of all success—in business, in the arts and in the home.

———

Joy

We do not know how cheap the seeds of happiness are or we should scatter them oftener.

———

To speak kindly does not hurt the tongue.

———

The nearer she approached the end, the plainer she seemed to hear round her the immortal symphonies of the world to come.

———

Dwell on the Duty of Happiness as well as the Happiness of Duty.

———

No man ever injured his eyesight by looking on the bright side of things.

———

Happiness is the only thing we can give without having.

———

There is no cosmetic for beauty like happiness.

———

The secret of contentment is knowing how to enjoy what you have and be able to lose all desire for things beyond your reach.

———

Do not speak of your happiness to one less fortunate than yourself.

———

Happiness is not a station you arrive at, but a manner of traveling.

———

You can't keep trouble from coming, but you needn't give it a chair to sit on.

———

Success is getting what you want; Happiness is wanting what you get.

———

Many of us spend half our time wishing for things we could have if we didn't spend half our time wishing.

———

All the flowers of all the tomorrows are in the seeds of today.

———

Joy

Defeat isn't bitter if you don't swallow it.

———

The deeper that sorrow carves into your being, the more joy you can contain.

———

The way to be happy is to make others happy.

———

The blue of heaven is larger than the clouds.

———

I should like to spend the whole of my life traveling, if I could anywhere borrow another life to live at home.

———

It is when the holiday is over that we begin to enjoy it.

———

The light that shines the farthest shines the brightest nearest home.

———

The happiness of your life depends upon the quality of your thoughts.

———

The glory of life is to love, not to be
loved; to give, not to get; to serve, not to
be served.

———

> Pleasures are like poppies spread;
> You seize the flower, the bloom is
> shed.

———

One of the biggest thrills in life comes
from doing a job well.

———

Each new days is an opportunity to start
all over again . . . to cleanse our minds
and hearts anew and to clarify our vision.
And let us not clutter up today with the
leavings of other days.

∽

Peace

Take with you words, strong words
    of courage:
Words that have wings! . . .
Take with you holy words, words
    that know God;
Words that are sacred as healing
    waters,
Pure as light, and beautiful as
    morning,
Take with you tall words, words that
    reach up,
And growing words, with deep life
    within them.
Take with you holy words, words
    that know God.

———

In His will is our peace.

———

If there is righteousness in the heart,
　there will be beauty in the
　　character,
If there is beauty in the character,
　there will be harmony in the home.
If there is harmony in the home,
　there will be order in the nation,
If there is order in the nation,
　There will be peace in the world.

———

Man's capacity for justice makes
democracy possible; but man's
inclination to injustice makes democracy
necessary.

———

Fear God and all other fears will
disappear.

———

In much of my talking, thinking is
half-murdered.

———

If you clutter up your mind with little
things, will there be any room left for the
big things?

———

Peace

We can never herd the world into the paths of righteousness with the dogs of war.

———

If humanity could be taught self-control and selfishness-control, there would be no need for atom control.

———

You are none the holier for being praised, and none the worse for being blamed.

———

You can't get anywhere today if you are still mired down in yesterday.

———

The load of tomorrow added to that of yesterday, carried today, makes the strongest falter.

———

Worry is interest paid on trouble before it is due.

———

Reality may be a rough road, but escape is a precipice.

———

Nothing in life is to be feared. It is only to be understood.

———

He that goes a borrowing goes a sorrowing.

———

That man is the richest whose pleasures are the cheapest.

———

The Bible is the book of all others to be read at all ages and in all conditions of human life.

———

Work is the best narcotic.

———

Habit is man's best friend or his worst enemy.

———

Quiet minds cannot be perplexed or frightened but go on in fortune or in misfortune at their own private pace like the ticking of a clock during a thunderstorm.

———

Peace

Our restlessness is largely due to the fact that we are as yet wanderers between two worlds.

——

Who is wise? He that learns from everyone.
Who is powerful? He that governs his passions.
Who is rich? He that is content.
Who is that? Nobody.

——

The fellow who worries about what people think of him wouldn't worry so much if he only knew how seldom they do.

——

Absence of occupation is not rest;
A mind quite vacant is a mind distressed.

——

He only is advancing in life whose heart is getting softer, his blood warmer, his brain quicker, and his spirit entering into living peace.

——

No wise man ever wished to be younger.

———

A clean conscience is a soft pillow.

———

All the sleepless nights, burdened days,
joyless, restless, peace-destroying,
health-destroying, happiness-destroying,
love-destroying hours men and women
have ever in all earth's centuries given to
Worry never wrought one good thing!

———

He who is taught to live upon little owes
more to his father's wisdom than he who
has a great deal left him does to his
father's care.

———

When you can no longer dwell in the
solitude of your heart, you live in your
lips and sound is a diversion and a
pastime.

———

Worry never climbed a hill
Worry never paid a bill
Worry never dried a tear

Peace

> Worry never calmed a fear
> Worry never darned a heel
> Worry never cooked a meal
> Worry never led a horse to water
> Worry never done a thing you'd
>   think it oughta.

―――

There is no conflict between the *old* and the *new*; the conflict is between the *false* and the *true*.

―――

It's right to be contented with what you have but never with what you are.

―――

> There is no place to hide a sin,
> Without the conscience looking in!

―――

Peace is not the absence of conflict, but the ability to cope with it.

―――

The rest of our days depends upon the rest of our nights.

―――

Anger is a wind which blows out the lamp of the mind.

―――

Though we travel the world over to find the beautiful, we must carry it with us or we find it not.

———

Rest is not quitting the busy career;
Rest is the fitting of self to its sphere.
'Tis loving and serving the highest
    and best!
'Tis onward unswerving, and that is
    true rest.

———

Are you disillusioned with your disillusionments?

———

Life is a voyage in which we choose neither vessel nor weather, but much can be done in the management of the sails and the guidance of the helm.

———

A good memory is fine—but the ability to forget is the true test of greatness.

———

The light that shows us our sin is the light that heals us.

———

Peace

God grant me the serenity to accept the things I cannot change; the courage to change the things I can; and the wisdom to know the difference.

———

To will what God wills brings peace.

———

Climb the mountains and get their glad tidings. Nature's peace will flow to you as the sunshine flows into the trees. The winds blow their own freshness into you, and the storms their energy, while cares drop away from you like the leaves of autumn.

———

Not even the perpetually hungry live by bread alone.

———

Solitude is the ante-chamber of God; only one step more and you will be in His immediate presence.

———

Any housewife, no matter how large her family, can always get some time to be alone by doing the dishes.

———

54

Great people are not affected by each puff of wind that blows ill. Like great ships, they sail serenely on, in a calm sea or a great tempest.

———

If you have known how to compose your life, you have accomplished a great deal more than a man who knows how to compose a book. Have you been able to take your stride? You have done more than the man who has taken cities and empires.

———

Meditation or Medication?

———

Pray or be a prey—a prey to fears, to futilities, to ineffectiveness.

———

You talk when you cease to be at peace with your thoughts.

———

A minute of thought is worth more than an hour of talk.

———

Peace

The itching sensation that some people mistake for ambition is merely inflammation of the wishbone.

————

To be content with little is difficult, to be content with much, impossible.

〰

Long suffering

Much wisdom remains to be learned, and if it is only to be learned through adversity, we must endeavor to endure adversity with what fortitude we can command. But if we can acquire wisdom soon enough, adversity may not be necessary and the future of man may be happier than any part of his past.

———

Education is a companion which no misfortune can decrease, no crime destroy, no enemy alienate, no despotism enslave; at home a friend, abroad an introduction, in solitude a solace, in society an ornament. It chastens vice, guides virtue, and gives grace and government to genius. Education may cost financial sacrifice and mental pain, but in both money and life values it will repay every cost one hundred fold.

———

There is a field for critics, no doubt, but we don't remember seeing statues of any of them in the Hall of Fame.

———

Why must we have memory enough to recall to the tiniest detail what has happened to us, and not enough to remember how many times we have told it to the same person.

———

The bird with a broken pinion never soared so high again, but its song is sweeter!

———

Whoever has resigned himself to fate, will find that fate, accepts his resignation.

———

One of the hardest things to teach our children about money matters is that it does.

———

If you have learned to walk
A little more sure-footedly than I,
Be patient with my stumbling then
And know that only as I do my best
    and try
May I attain the goal
For which we both are striving.

If through experience, your soul
Has gained heights which I
As yet in dim-lit vision see,
Hold out your hand and point the
    way,
Lest from its straightness I should
    stray,
And walk a mile with me.

———

Men and automobiles are much alike.
Some are right at home on an uphill pull;
others run smoothly only going
down-grade, and when you hear one
knocking all the time, it's a sure sign
there is something wrong under the
hood.

———

59

Long suffering

Charity is injurious unless it helps the recipient to become independent of it.

———

We can do anything we want if we stick to it long enough.

———

What we do not understand we do not possess.

———

Will Power—Won't Power—Supreme Power!

———

If you never stick your neck out, you'll never get your head above the crowd.

———

Patience—in time the grass becomes milk.

———

There is no sense in advertising your troubles. There's no market for them.

———

Genius is only patience.

———

He who accepts evil without protesting against it is really cooperating with it.

———

A man could retire nicely in his old age if he could dispose of his experience for what it cost him.

———

It is not the ship in the water but the water in the ship that sinks it.

———

It is not miserable to be blind; it is miserable to be incapable of enduring blindness.

———

You cannot help men permanently by doing for them what they could and should do for themselves.

———

Fortune does not change men. It only unmasks them.

———

Use disappointment as material for patience.

———

Long suffering

Telling your troubles always helps. The world's dumb indifference makes you mad enough to keep on fighting.

———

Women are here to stay . . .
let's make the best of them.

———

Those who have suffered much are like those who know many languages; they have learned to understand all and to be understood by all.

———

The worst thing that happens to a man may be the best thing that ever happened to him if he doesn't let it get the best of him.

———

There is no failure save in giving up.

———

Sometimes the best gain is to lose.

———

A man can fail many times, but he isn't a failure until he begins to blame somebody else.

———

Forget mistakes. Organize victory out of mistakes.

———

All problems become smaller if you don't dodge them but confront them. Touch a thistle timidly and it will prick you; grasp it boldly and its spines crumble.

———

He who strikes the first blow confesses he has run out of ideas.

———

A man's best fortune or his worst is his wife.

———

When you're through changing, you're through.

———

The diamond cannot be polished without friction, nor man perfected without trials.

———

Trying times are times for trying.

———

Long suffering

Education should be as gradual as the moonrise, perceptible not in progress but in result.

———

Why value the present hour less than some future hour?

———

The secret of patience is doing something else in the meanwhile.

———

If you don't scale the mountain, you can't see the view.

———

Trouble is only opportunity in work clothes.

———

Only one person in the whole wide world can defeat you. That is yourself!

———

> Like a hick'ry cog
> In the old mill wheel,
> He did his part
> As his turn came 'round.

———

I had no shoes and complained until I
met a man who had no feet.

———

Before you flare up at any one's faults,
take time to count ten—ten of your own.

———

We are never more discontented with
others than when we are discontented
with ourselves.

———

The door to the room of success swings
on the hinges of opposition.

———

It isn't the load that weights us
down—it's the way we carry it.

———

The greatest calamity is not to have
failed; but to have failed to try.

———

The only time you mustn't fail is the last
time you try.

———

A diamond is a piece of coal that stuck to
the job.

———

Long suffering

God never makes us conscious of our weakness except to give us of His strength.

———

There is nothing wrong with the younger generation that twenty years won't cure.

———

Stars may be seen from the bottom of a deep well, when they cannot be seen from the top of the mountain. So are many things learned in adversity, which the prosperous man dreams not of.

———

Perhaps the most valuable result of all education is the *ability* to make ourselves do the thing we have to do *when* it ought to be done, whether we like it or not.

———

The hardest thing of all in life—
  The conquest not of time and
    space,
But of ourselves, of our stupidity and
    inertia,

of our greediness and touchiness,
Of our fear and intolerant
dogmatism.

———

The difference between stumbling
blocks and stepping stones is the way a
man uses them.

———

Every time you give another a "piece of
your mind" you add to your own
vacuum.

———

We cannot do everything at once; but we
can do something at once.

———

No horse gets anywhere till he is
harnessed.
No steam ever drives anything until it is
confined.
No Niagara is ever turned into light and
power until it is tunneled.
No life ever grows great until it is
focused, dedicated, disciplined.

———

Long suffering

A mistake is evidence that someone has tried to do something.

———

When the archer misses the center of the target he seeks for the cause within himself.

———

The world is made better by every man improving his own conduct; and no reform is accomplished wholesale.

———

The most difficult year of marriage is the one you're in.

———

Life is 10% what you make it and 90% how you take it.

———

Be not angry that you cannot make others as you wish them to be since you cannot make yourself as you wish to be.

———

Itching for what you want doesn't do much good; you've got to scratch for it.

———

He who has learned to disagree without being disagreeable has discovered the most valuable secret of a diplomat.

———

Your ulcers are not due to what you are eatin' but to what's eatin' you.

———

Better to let 'em wonder why you didn't talk than why you did.

———

We would rather be ruined by praise than saved by criticism.

———

If at first you don't succeed, you are running about average.

———

Do not be disturbed at being misunderstood. Be disturbed only at not understanding.

———

> Our Country, right or wrong!
> When right, to be kept right;
> When wrong, to be put right.

———

Long suffering

You've reached middle age when all you exercise is caution.

―――――

It takes the whole of life to learn how to live.

―――――

Housework is something you do that nobody notices unless you don't do it.

―――――

It isn't the mountain ahead that wears you out—it's the grain of sand in your shoe.

―――――

The highest reward that God gives us for good work is the ability to do better.

―――――

Everything comes to him who waits, if he works while he waits.

―――――

Injustice is relatively easy to bear; what stings is justice.

―――――

Do not go to pieces if you burn the toast. Some day your house may burn down and you can take that calmly too.

―――――

Marrying is not Marriage.

———

No one can work me injury but myself.

———

To be thrown upon one's resources is to be cast into the very lap of fortune.

———

The trouble with some people is that they won't admit their faults. I'd admit mine—if I had any.

———

The Lord sometimes takes us into troubled waters NOT to drown us, but to cleanse us.

———

Try to fix the mistake—never the blame.

———

To sin by silence when they should protest, makes cowards of men.

———

The world is not interested in the storms you encountered—but did you bring in the ship?

———

Long suffering

I'd better not be wasting Time,
For Time is wasting me!

———

Just about the time you think you can make both ends meet, somebody moves the ends.

———

Education isn't play and it can't be made to look like play. It is hard, hard work, but it can be made interesting work.

———

Talent may develop in solitude, but character is developed in society.

———

The more difficult the obstacle, the stronger one becomes after hurdling it.

———

Tact is the ability to close your mouth before someone else wants to.

———

Fault finders never improve the world; they only make it seem worse than it really is.

———

Don't tell your friends about your
indigestion:
"How are you" is a *greeting,* not a
question.

———

No difficulties, no discovery,
No pains, no gains.

———

Taxes could be much worse—suppose
we had to pay on what we *think* we're
worth.

———

A failure is a man who has blundered but
is not able to cash in the experience.

———

Failure is endeavor, and endeavor
persisted in, is never failure.

———

One thing at a time and that done
well
is a very good rule as many can tell.

———

Help me never to judge another until I
have walked two weeks in his shoes.

———

Long suffering

Learn from the mistakes of others—you can't live long enough to make them all yourself.

∽

Gentleness

This book can be like a well-chosen and well-tended fruit tree. Its fruits are not of one season only. With the due and natural intervals, you may recur to it year after year, and it will supply the same nourishment and the same gratification, if only you return to it with the same healthy appetite.

———

So many Gods, so many creeds,
So many paths that wind and wind;
When just the art of being kind
Is all the sad world needs.

———

If you have a weakness, make it work for you as a strength—and if you have a strength, don't abuse it into a weakness.

———

Gentleness

The kindly word that falls today may bear its fruit tomorrow.

———

A good manner springs from a good heart, and fine manners are the outcome of unselfish kindness.

———

One cannot find any rule of conduct to excel "simplicity" and "sincerity."

———

To speak kindly does not hurt the tongue.

———

Every noble life leaves the fibre of it interwoven in the woof of the world.

———

He who influences the thought of his time influences the thought of all the times that follow.

———

The blossom cannot tell what becomes of its odor and no man can tell what becomes of his influence and example that roll away from him and go beyond his view.

———

Only the best behavior is good enough
for daily use in the home.

———

True nobility comes of the gentle heart.

———

Prejudice is being down on what we are
not up on.

———

Nothing is so strong as gentleness,
nothing so gentle as real strength.

———

A candle-glow can pierce the darkest
night.

———

A gentleman is a gentle man.

———

Speech may sometimes do harm; but so
may silence and a worse harm at that. No
insult ever caused so deep a wound as a
tenderness expected and withheld; and
no spoken indiscretion was ever so
bitterly regretted as the word that one
did not speak.

———

Gentleness

Be what you wish others to become.

———

Kindness is a language the dumb can speak and the deaf understand.

———

> Be to his virtues very kind.
> Be to his faults a little blind.

———

One learns manners from those who have none.

———

An admission of error is a sign of strength rather than a confession of weakness.

———

If you confer a benefit, never remember it; If you receive one, never forget it.

———

Be kind, for everyone you meet is fighting a hard battle.

∽

Goodness

We are all manufacturers, making goods, making trouble or making excuses.

———

A little thing is a little thing, but faithfulness in little things is a great thing.

———

Character is property—it is the noblest of possessions.

———

The highest reward for a man's toil is not what he gets for it, but rather what he becomes by it.

———

It is not so much what a man is descended from that matters as what he will descend to.

———

Goodness

Truth is the foundation of all knowledge and the cement of all societies.

———

You can preach a better sermon with your life than with your lips.

———

Praise not only pretends that we are better than we are; it may help to make us better than we are.

———

Good depends not on things but on the use we make of things.

———

Resolve to be better for the echo of it.

———

If anyone speaks evil of you, so live that none will believe it.

———

Life is too short to be little.

———

To the man in us, time is a quantity; To the God in us, it is a quality.

———

To do the right thing for the wrong
reason is the greatest treason.

Who worships Christ in bread and
     wine,
   And kneels before the High and
     Pure,
   Meets Him again in street and mine
   And in the faces of the poor.

We've got to build a better man before
we build a better society.

You are writing a gospel,
A chapter each day,
By deeds that you do,
By words that you say.
Men read what you write,
Whether faithless or true,
Say, what is the gospel according to
     you?

The only way to settle a disagreement is
on the basis of what's right—not who's
right.

Goodness

What I must do, and not what people think, is all that concerns me.

———

Silver and gold are not the only coin; virtue also passes all over the world.

———

Your luck is how you treat people.

———

The measure of man's real character is what he would do if he knew he would never be found out.

———

See each person you meet as one who knows your Lord or is seeking your Lord.

———

To every man there opens a high way and a low and every man decides the way that he shall go.

———

We search the world for truth, we
    cull
The good, the true, the beautiful,

From graven stone and written
    scroll,
And all old flower-fields of the soul;
And, weary seekers of the best,
We come back laden from our quest,
To find that all the sages said
Is in the Book our mothers read.

————

We have committed the Golden Rule to
memory; let us now commit it to life.

————

The greatest distance we have yet to
cover still lies within us.

————

A man is rich according to what he is,
not according to what he has.

————

A good example is the best sermon.

————

The world is slowly learning that because
two men think differently neither need
be wicked.

————

Goodness

The Golden Rule—not the rule of gold.

———

Children need models more than they need critics.

———

Life lived just to satisfy yourself never satisfies anybody.

———

There is no better exercise for strengthening the heart than reaching down and lifting people up.

———

What lies behind us and what lies before us are tiny matters compared to what lies within us.

———

Character is a victory, not a gift.

———

There is no right way to do the wrong thing.

———

Whatever creed be taught or land be trod,
Man's conscience is the oracle of God.

———

What I am to be I am now becoming.

———

The hardest job that people have to do is
to move religion from their throats to
their muscles.

———

A living religion is a way of living.

———

A man's reputation is only what men
think him to be; his character is what
God knows him to be.

———

Goodness is the only investment that
never fails.

———

Though another may have more money,
beauty, brains than you; yet when it
comes to the rarer spiritual values such
as charity, self-sacrifice, honor, nobility
of heart, you have an equal chance with
everyone to be the most beloved and
honored of all people.

———

Goodness

The real purpose of our existence is not to make a living, but to make a life—a worthy, well-rounded, useful life.

> Do all the good you can
> By all the means you can
> In all the ways you can
> In all the places you can
> At all the times you can
> To all the people you can
> As long as ever you can.

Christian character is not an inheritance; each individual must build it for himself.

What you are in the sight of God, that you truly are.

To clear difficulties out of the way, there is no axe like a good principle.

Are you easing the load of overtaxed lifters who toil down the road? Or, are you a leaner who lets others share your portion of labor, worry and care?

Good nature will always supply the absence of beauty; but beauty cannot supply the absence of good nature.

———

Be careful how you live; you may be the only Bible some people will ever read.

———

Be the true man you seek.

———

Nothing which is morally wrong can ever be politically right.

———

My part is to improve the present moment.

———

Do right and leave the results with God.

———

The difference between a prejudice and a conviction is that you can explain a conviction without getting mad.

———

To become Christlike is the only thing in the whole world worth caring for; the thing before which every ambition of man is folly, and all lower achievement vain.

———

It will not be easy to brainwash the heartwashed.

———

Democracy means not "I am equal to you" but "you are equal to me."

———

Life is not the wick or the candle—it is the burning.

———

It is often surprising to find what heights may be attained merely by remaining on the level.

———

It is as hard for the good to suspect evil as it is for the bad to suspect good.

———

> For when the One Great Scorer
>   comes,
>   To write against your name,
> He writes not that you lost or won,
>   But how you played the game.

———

All that is necessary for the triumph of evil is that good men do nothing.

———

The Devil has many tools, but a lie is the handle that fits them all.

———

Know enough to, know enough not to.

———

If you blame others for your failures, do you credit others with your successes?

———

There isn't any map on the *road* to *success;* you have to find your own way.

———

He who is not liberal with what he has deceives himself when he thinks he would be liberal if he had more.

———

Are you trying to make something for yourself or something of yourself?

———

A lie has no legs. It requires other lies to support it. Tell one lie and you are forced to tell others to back it up.

———

Goodness

A good man does not hesitate to own he has been in the wrong. He takes comfort in knowing he is wiser today than he was yesterday.

———

Stretching the truth won't make it last any longer.

———

The only wise speed at which to live is . . . Godspeed.

———

I have resolved never to do anything which I should be afraid to do if it were the last hour of my life.

౭

Faith

Faith is a gift of God. It is not a material that can be seen, heard, smelled, tasted, or touched; but is as real as anything that can be perceived with these senses. One can be aware of Faith as easily as one can be aware of earth. Faith is as certain as is the existence of water. Faith is as sure as the taste of an apple, the fragrance of a rose, the sound of thunder, the sight of the sun, the feel of a loving touch.

Hope is a wish, a longing for something not now possessed, but with the expectation of getting it.

Faith adds surety to the expectation of hope.

―――――

Today is the tomorrow you worried about yesterday.

―――――

Faith

I am to be so busy today that I must spend more time than usual in prayer.

————

Inexperience is what makes a young man do what an older man says is impossible.

————

When you get to the end of your rope, tie a knot in it and hang on.

————

You are not a reservoir with a limited amount of resources; you are a channel attached to unlimited divine resources.

————

God is playing chess with man. He meets his every move.

————

The sectarian thinks that he has the sea ladled into his private pond.

————

Who draws nigh to God through doubtings dim . . . God will advance a mile in blazing light to him.

————

I am only one, but I am one. I cannot do everything, but I can do something; and what I should do and can do, by the Grace of God I will do.

———

No vision and you perish
No ideal and you are lost,
Your heart must ever cherish
Some faith at any cost.

———

Anyone can carry his burden, however heavy, until nightfall; anyone can do his work, however hard, for one day.

———

Prayer is not overcoming God's reluctance; it is laying hold on His willingness.

———

Prayer is not an attitude attained but an attitude maintained.

———

The secret of prayer is secret prayer.

———

Faith

The man who trusts men will make fewer mistakes than he who distrusts them.

———

God's requirements are met by God's enablings.

———

A skeptic is one who won't take *know* for an answer.

———

I have faith in Him, not in my faith.

———

No man is responsible for the rightness of his faith; but only for the uprightness of it.

———

Dare to be wise; begin! He who postpones the hour of living rightly is like the rustic who waits for the river to run out before he crosses.

———

The night is not forever.

———

Do not worry about whether or not the sun will rise; be prepared to enjoy it.

———

The best and most beautiful things in the world cannot be seen nor touched but are felt in the heart.

———

The Christian on his knees sees more than the philosopher on tiptoe.

———

Nothing costs so much as what is bought by prayers.

———

It is better to suffer wrong than to do it, and happier to sometimes be cheated than not to trust.

———

God never closes one door without opening another.

———

Faith is the grave of care.

———

Prayer is not a substitute for work. It is a desperate effort to work further and to be effective beyond the range of one's power.

———

Faith

We are always complaining our days are few, and acting as though there would be no end of them.

―――

The past cannot be changed; the future is still in your power.

―――

O, Lord, help me to understand that you ain't gwine to let nuthin' come my way that you and me together can't handle.

―――

> What you can do, or dream you can,
>   begin it.
> Courage has genius, power and magic
>   in it;
> Only engage, and then the mind
>   grows heated.
> Begin it and the work will be
>   completed.

―――

Some people can see at a glance what others cannot see with searchlights and telescopes.

―――

The best evidence of the Bible's being the Word of God is to be found between its covers.

———

Life is easier than you think. All you have to do is accept the impossible, do without the indispensable, and bear the intolerable.

———

Prayer without work is beggary;
Work without prayer is slavery.

———

What are you saving in your memory bin as food for the restless soul when the winter of life comes?

———

I'll take the Bible as my guide until something better comes along.

———

For a web begun, God sends thread.

———

Life is eternal, Love is immortal and Death is only an horizon, and an horizon is only the limit of our sight.

———

Faith

Instead of waiting upon the Lord, some people want the Lord to wait upon them.

———

This body is my house—it is not I.
Triumphant in this faith I live and
die.

———

Satan trembles when he sees the weakest saint upon his knees.

———

To pray "Thy will be done" should be no attitude of passive submission but a call to the whole nature to strive to do the utmost for the cause of God.

———

With God, go even over the sea;
Without Him, not over the
threshold.

———

With God, nothing shall be impossible.

———

It is not the lazy who are most inclined to prayer; those pray most who care most, and who, having worked hard, find it intolerable to be defeated.

———

Don't tell me that worry doesn't do any good. I know better. The things I worry about don't happen.

———

If a man has any religion, he must give it up or give it away.

———

Do the very best you can . . . and leave the outcome to God.

———

I know not what the future hath of marvel or surprise, assured alone that life and death His mercy underlies.

———

The trival round, our common task,
    Would furnish all we ought to ask;
Room to deny ourselves; a road
    to bring us daily nearer God.

———

Real prayer always does one of two things: It either frees us from the trouble we fear or else it gives us the strength and courage to meet the trouble when it comes.

———

Faith

One on God's side is a majority.

———

Are your troubles causing you to lose
your religion or use your religion?

———

Wit's end need not be the end, but the
beginning. The end of man's contriving
often is the beginning of God's arriving.

———

Life left to God
Will bring a greater yield
Of golden harvest and of ripened field
Than all the weary plannings of thy soul
Can force to be, or strength of will
    control;
Oh, trust a Power than must bring good
    from all,
And leave thy life to God!

———

If a psychologist assures me that I believe
in God because of the way my nurse used
to treat me, I must reply that he only
holds that belief concerning my belief
because of the way in which his nurse
used to treat him.

———

Why is it opportunities always look bigger going than coming?

———

All I see teaches me to trust the Creator for all I do not see.

———

If seeds in the black earth can turn into such beautiful roses, what might not the heart of man become in its long journey toward the stars?

———

> Of all the troubles great and small
> are those that never happened at all.

———

The Bible is a guidebook; the way to master it is to let it master us.

———

Freedom rests, and always will, on individual responsibility, individual integrity, individual effort, individual courage, and individual religious faith.

———

Man's extremity is God's opportunity.

———

Faith

If there is no way out, there is a way up.

———

This is what I found out about religion:
It gives you courage to make the
decisions you must make in a crisis, and
then the confidence to leave the result to
a *higher power.* Only by trust in God can
a man carrying responsibility find
repose.

———

A wish is a desire without any attempt to
attain its end.

———

It is difficult to pray because it is difficult
to know what we ought to desire.

———

It is only the fear of God that can deliver
us from the fear of men.

———

Morale is when your hands and feet keep
on working when your head says it can't
be done.

———

Death is not extinguishing the light; it is putting out the lamp because dawn has come.

———

Out of the seed the flower;
    Out of the flower the seed;
Out of the need the power;
    Out of the power the deed.

———

Only he who can see the invisible can do the impossible.

———

Do you pray, and then believing,
    Grab your boots and parasol;
Scrub the barrel and *get ready*
    For the rain you asked to fall?

———

Don't be afraid to be afraid.

———

He says not, "at the end of the *way* you find ME." He says, "I AM the *way*: I AM the road under your feet, the road that begins just as low as you happen to be."

———

Faith

Be patient enough to live one day at a time as Jesus taught us, letting yesterday go and leaving tomorrow until it arrives.

———

Instead of fearing death, we should look it in the face and recognize it for what it is—a friend that has come to release us from the bondage of the flesh.

———

Lord, I shall be very busy this day. I may forget thee . . . But do not Thou forget me.

———

We plant a tree this day and leave the blossoming to God.

———

Fear brings more pain than does the pain it fears.

———

All the fitness He requireth is to feel your need of Him.

———

Does your faith move mountains, or do mountains move your faith?

———

Prayer should be the key of the day and the lock of the night.

———

Do you have invisible means of support?

———

Our doubts are traitors and make us lose the good oft we might win, by fearing to attempt.

———

Life is real! Life is earnest!
And the grave is not its goal;
Dust thou art, to dust returnest,
Was not spoken of the soul.

———

If you must doubt, doubt your doubts—never your beliefs.

———

A man is not old until regrets take the place of dreams.

———

Cease to inquire what the future has in store, but take as a gift whatever the day brings forth.

———

Faith

Nothing is all wrong. Even a clock that has stopped running is right twice a day.

———

No worlds left to conquer? The frontiers of the mind are just beginning to be discovered, and the spiritual world surrounding us yet remains a complete mystery.

———

First do more than you are paid for before expecting to be paid for more than you do.

———

Prayer digs the channels from the reservoir of God's boundless resources to the tiny pools of our lives.

———

There is no greater obstacle in the way of success in life than trusting for something to turn up, instead of going to work and turning up something.

———

I never knew a night so black
Light failed to follow on its track.

I never knew a storm so gray,
It failed to have its clearing day.
I never knew such bleak despair,
That there was not a rift, somewhere.
I never knew an hour so drear,
Love could not fill it full of cheer.

———

Some folks just don't seem to realize
when they're moaning about not getting
prayers answered, that NO is the
answer.

———

Life is hard, by the yard;
But by the inch, *life's* a cinch!

———

The task of spiritual science: Discover
the little acorns out of which big oaks
grow and provide room for the growth of
such mighty trees.

———

We can easily forgive a child who is
afraid of the dark. The real tragedy of
life is when men are afraid of the Light.

———

Faith

Without the *way*, there is no going;
Without the *truth*, there is no
    knowing;
Without the *life*, there is no living.

The world is moved not only by the
mighty shoves of the heroes, but also by
the aggregate of the tiny pushes of each
honest worker.

He didn't know it couldn't be done but
went ahead and did it.

A Traveler crossed a frozen stream
    In trembling fear one day;
Later a teamster drove across,
    And whistled all the way.

Great faith and little faith alike
    Were granted safe convoy;
One had the pangs of needless fear,
    The other all the joy.

It is not the greatness of my faith that

moves mountains, but my faith in the greatness of God.

———

You can't control the length of your life—but you can control its width and depth. You can't control the contour of your face—but you can control its expression. You can't control the weather—but you can control the atmosphere of your mind. Why worry about things you can't control when you can keep yourself busy controlling the things that depend on you.

———

People believe what they want to believe despite all the evidence to the contrary.

———

As is your "Amen" so is your prayer.

———

Prayer changes things. Prayer changes you!

———

He who loses money loses much;
he who loses a friend loses more,
but he who loses *faith* loses all.

———

Faith

The only ideas that will work for you are
the ones you put to work.

———

  God without man is still God.
  Man without God is nothing.

———

When we see the lilies spinning in
  distress,
Taking thought to manufacture
  loveliness—
When we see the birds all building barns
  for store,
'Twill be time for us to worry, not
  before.

∽

Meekness

Have courage to be ignorant of a great number of things, in order to avoid the calamity of being ignorant of everything.

——

The only conquests which are permanent, and leave no regrets, are conquests over ourselves.

——

Resiliency is an important factor in living. The winds of life may bend us, but if we have resilience of spirit, they cannot break us. To courageously straighten again after our heads have been bowed by defeat, disappointment and suffering is the supreme test of character.

——

Meekness

To know how to grow old is the master work of wisdom, and one of the most difficult chapters in the great art of living.

———

The best medicine for you to take is yourself—with a grain of salt.

———

It is with narrow-souled people as with narrow necked bottles—the less they have in them the more noise they make in pouring it out.

———

There is only one person with whom you can profitably compare yourself, and this person is your yesterday self: You

———

The greatest undeveloped territory in the world lies under your hat.

———

Discussion is an exchange of knowledge: argument is an exchange of ignorance.

———

Wisdom is to know what is best worth knowing and to do what is best worth doing.

_____

Some husbands know all the answers. They've been listening for years.

_____

If we resist our passions, it is more through their weakness than our strength.

_____

Conscience is the still small voice that makes you feel still smaller.

_____

The doorstep to the temple of wisdom is a knowledge of our own ignorance.

_____

To be conscious that you are ignorant is a great step toward knowledge.

_____

Never forget that you are a part of the people who can be fooled some of the time.

_____

Meekness

Don't drive as if you own the road; Drive as if you own the car.

———

Teach thy tongue to say, "I do not know."

———

A juvenile delinquent is a boy who does what you did when young, but gets caught.

———

There is nothing permanent but change.

———

The best way to succeed in life is to act on the advice you give to others.

———

A peck of common sense is worth a bushel of learning.

———

The bigger a man's head gets, the easier it is to fill his shoes.

———

Past experience should be a guide post, not a hitching post.

———

The end of wisdom is to dream high enough not to lose the dream in the seeking of it.

_____

There's nothing wrong with being a self-made man if you don't consider the job finished too soon.

_____

The aim of education is to enable man to continue his learning.

_____

Life is like a ladder. Every step we take is either up or down.

_____

What a fool does in the end, the wise man does in the beginning.

_____

A college education seldom hurts a man if he's willing to learn a little something after he graduates.

_____

Swallowing your pride occasionally will never give you indigestion.

_____

Meekness

A philosopher is someone who always knows what to do until it happens to him.

———

I am not conceited, though I do have every reason to be.

———

The steam that blows the whistle can't be used to turn the wheels.

———

Manhood, not scholarship, is the first aim of education.

———

When success turns a person's head, he is facing failure.

———

Men are wise in proportion not to their experience but to their capacity for experience.

———

No experienced man ever stigmatized a change of opinion as inconsistency.

———

Education does not mean teaching people to know what they do not know; it means teaching them to behave as they do not behave.

———

Quite often when a man thinks his mind is getting broader it is only his conscience stretching.

———

Opinions that are well rooted should grow and change like a healthy tree.

———

Lord, give me this day my daily opinion, and forgive me the one I had yesterday.

———

I thoroughly believe in a university education for both men and women, but I believe a knowledge of the Bible without a college course is more valuable than a college course without a knowledge of the Bible.

———

Meekness

Many might have attained wisdom had they not thought that they had already attained it.

———

The taller a bamboo grows, the lower it bends.

———

A criminal is nothing else but you and me at our weakest, found out.

———

Seems as if some people grow with responsibility—others just swell.

———

Every man I meet is in some way my superior; and in that I can learn from him.

———

When you know a thing, to hold that you know it, and when you do not know it, to admit that you do not—this is true knowledge.

———

The more you know, the more you know you don't know.

———

To admit I have been in the wrong is but saying that I am wiser today than I was yesterday.

———

It makes a man sort of humble to have been a kid when everything was the kid's fault and a parent at a time when everything is the parent's fault.

———

> The greatest friend of truth is time,
> And her constant companion is
> humility.

———

When you hear that someone has gossiped of you, kindly reply that he did not know the rest of your faults or he would not have mentioned only these.

———

To err may be human, but to admit it isn't.

———

The purpose of education is to provide everyone with the opportunity to learn how best he may serve the world.

———

Meekness

Nothing gives a man more leisure time than being punctual.

———

A professor once said that it didn't matter if one said, "I seed," if one really had seen something.

———

Wisdom consists in knowing what to do with what you know.

———

A learned man has always wealth within himself.

———

Investment in knowledge pays the best interest.

———

The man who trims himself to suit everybody will soon whittle himself away.

———

The righteous cannot rise beyond the highest which is in me so the wicked and the weak cannot fall lower than the lowest in me.

———

Everyone is ignorant—only on different subjects.

_____

Humility is a strange thing. The minute you think you've got it, you've lost it.

_____

When young, consider that one day you will be old and when old, remember you were once young.

_____

A man wrapped up in himself makes a very small bundle.

_____

They that know God will be humble; they that know themselves cannot be proud.

_____

If you want to put the world right, start with yourself.

_____

It is indeed a desirable thing to be well descended, but the glory belongs to our ancestors.

_____

Meekness

A college graduate is a person who had a chance to get an education.

———

Tolerance comes with age. I see no fault committed that I myself could not have committed at some time or other.

———

The greatest of faults is to be conscious of none.

———

Nonchalance is the ability to look like an owl when you have acted like a jackass.

———

When a man gets too old to set a bad example, he starts giving good advice.

———

An open mind leaves a chance for someone to drop a worthwhile thought in it.

———

A diplomat is one who can tell a man he's open minded when he means he has a hole in his head.

———

We see things not as they are, but as we are.

———

The best thing for gray hair is a sensible head.

———

Time cannot be expanded, accumulated, mortgaged, hastened, or retarded.

———

Women will remain the weaker sex just as long as they're smarter.

———

It is my privilege to profit by the experience of others, but I must live my own life, face the trials, and gain the victory alone.

———

God never makes us sensible of our weakness except to give us of His strength.

———

Most people's hindsight is 20/20.

———

Meekness

Every other kind of iniquity prompts the doing of evil deeds, but pride lurks even in good deeds to their undoing.

———

Are you sure that you are Right?
How fine and strong!
But were you ever just as sure—
And wrong?

———

Flattery is something nice someone tells you about yourself that you wish were true.

———

It is better to understand a little than to misunderstand a lot.

∽

Temperance

Where there is an open mind, there will always be a frontier.

———

The longer you keep your temper the more it will improve.

———

It's smart to pick your friends—but not to pieces.

———

Fine eloquence consists in saying all that should be, not all that could be said.

———

Wise men are not always silent, but know when to be.

———

We always have time enough if we but use it aright.

———

Temperance

Spend less than you get.

———

Frugality is good if liberality be joined by it.

———

It's not that I spend more than I earn, it's just that I spend it quicker than I earn it.

———

There is only a slight difference between keeping your chin up and sticking your neck out, but it's worth knowing.

———

The hand that lifts "the cup that cheers" should not be used to shift the gears.

> The driver is safer when the roads are dry;
> the roads are safer when the driver is dry.

Be sure your brain is in gear before engaging your mouth.

———

Blessed is he who, having nothing to say, refrains from giving wordy evidence of the fact.

———

If your dollar won't do as much as it once did, consider: Are you doing as much as you once did for a dollar?

———

Laziness travels so slowly that poverty soon overtakes him.

———

A man's difficulties begin when he is able to do as he likes.

———

We cannot do everything at once; but we can do something at once.

———

As easy as falling off a diet.

———

Gossip is the art of saying nothing in a way that leaves nothing unsaid.

———

Words in haste do friendships waste.

———

Temperance

Silence is a talent as greatly to be cherished as that other asset, the gift of speech.

———

"A soft answer turneth away wrath" is the best system of self-defense.

———

People who fly into a rage always make a bad landing.

———

I'se alus mighty careful to stop and taste mah words 'fore I lets 'em pass mah teeth!

———

Often the difference between a successful marriage and a mediocre one consists of leaving about three or four things a day unsaid.

———

Will power is the ability to eat one salted peanut.

———

We need mental separators that take off the few ounces of cream which are fit to be spoken to others.

———

Tact is the unsaid part of what you think.

———

In any controversy the instant we feel anger we have already ceased striving for truth, and have begun striving for ourselves.

———

Thrift is a wonderful virtue—especially in ancestors.

———

It is better to keep your mouth shut and thought a fool than it is to open it and prove it.

———

The best victory is to conquer self.

———

Dignity is the capacity to hold back on the tongue what never should have been in the mind in the first place.

———

Temperance

To cease smoking is the easiest thing I ever did. I ought to know for I've done it a thousand times.

——

Habit is a cable; we weave a thread of it every day, and at last we cannot break it.

——

Choose the best life, for habit will make it pleasant.

——

Seconds count, especially when dieting.

——

The test of good manners is being able to put up pleasantly with bad ones.

——

In times of crisis we must avoid both ignorant change and ignorant opposition to change.

——

Best rule I know for talkin' is the same as the one for carpenterin': Measure twice and saw once.

——

Even moderation ought not to be practiced to excess.

——

Out of the mouths of babes come words we shouldn't have said in the first place.

_____

You can never tell about a woman, and if you can, you shouldn't.

_____

Who gossips to you will gossip of you.

_____

The real problem of your leisure is how to keep other people from using it.

_____

Better to slip with the foot than with the tongue.

_____

The archer who overshoots his mark does no better than he who falls short of it.

_____

Economy is an important virtue and debt can be a danger to be feared.

_____

Besides the noble art of getting things done, there is the noble art of leaving things undone.

Temperance

The wisdom of life consists in the elimination of nonessentials.

———

Do you act or react?

———

We always weaken what we exaggerate.

———

There is nothing wrong with making mistakes, but don't respond to encores.

———

Your body is for use—not abuse.

———

If silence be good for wise men, how much better must it be for fools.

———

Do you spend more than you make on things you don't need to impress people you don't like?

———

No echoes return to mock the silent tongue.

———

I have often regretted my speech, seldom my silence.

———

It's all right to hold a conversation, but you should let go of it now and then.

———

If your outgo exceeds your income, then your upkeep will be your downfall.

———

Man is master of the unspoken word, which, spoken, is master of him.

———

Speech is the index of the mind.

———

Overweight is often just desserts.

———

Money may not go as far as it used to, but we have just as much trouble getting it back.

———

A loose tongue often gets into a tight place.

———

Too many people quit looking for work when they find a job.

———

Temperance

Ideas are funny little things. They won't work unless you do.

———

Sooner throw a pearl at hazard than an idle or useless word; and do not say a little in many words, but a great deal in a few.

Everything has been thought of before . . .
the difficulty is to think of it again.

134